D0460859

AMERICAN CITIZENSHIP

VOTING AND ELECTIONS

by Kate Conley

Content Consultant
Richard Bell
Associate Professor, Department of History
University of Maryland

Core Library

An Imprint of Abdo Publishing
abdopublishing.com

abdopublishing.com

Published by Abdo Publishing, a division of ABDO, PO Box 398166, Minneapolis, Minnesota 55439. Copyright © 2017 by Abdo Consulting Group, Inc. International copyrights reserved in all countries. No part of this book may be reproduced in any form without written permission from the publisher. Core Library™ is a trademark and logo of Abdo Publishing.

Printed in the United States of America, North Mankato, Minnesota
042016
092016

THIS BOOK CONTAINS
RECYCLED MATERIALS

Cover Photo: Reed Saxon/AP Images
Interior Photos: Reed Saxon/AP Images, 1; Tamir Kalifa/AP Images, 4, 45; Ohio Statehouse, 7; Ann Hermes/The Christian Science Monitor/Getty Images, 9; Corbis, 12; Red Line Editorial, 15, 30; Nam Y. Huh/AP Images, 17; David Paul Morris/Bloomberg/Getty Images, 20, 43; David Paul Morris/Bloomberg/Getty Images, 23; Randy Duchaine/Alamy, 24; J. Scott Applewhite/AP Images, 28; Helen H. Richardson/The Denver Post/Getty Images, 34; Library of Congress, 37; Bill Pugliano/Getty Images, 40

Editor: Sharon F. Doorasamy
Series Designer: Laura Polzin

Cataloging-in-Publication Data
Names: Conley, Kate, author.
Title: Voting and elections / by Kate Conley.
Description: Minneapolis, MN : Abdo Publishing, [2017] | Series: American
    citizenship | Includes bibliographical references and index.
Identifiers: LCCN 2015960489 | ISBN 9781680782448 (lib. bdg.) |
    ISBN 9781680776553 (ebook)
Subjects: LCSH: Political campaigns--United States--Juvenile literature. |
     Politics, practical--United States--Juvenile literature. | Voting--United States--
    Juvenile literature. | Elections--United States--Juvenile literature. | United
    States--Politics and government--Juvenile literature.
Classification: DDC 324--dc23
LC record available at http://lccn.loc.gov/2015960489

CONTENTS

CHAPTER ONE

CHOOSING OUR LEADERS

Election Day is an important event in the United States. On this day, citizens vote to elect their leaders. Voting is an important part of a democracy. A democracy is a system of government by the people. To vote is a responsibility of American citizenship.

US elections have a long, humble history. The first presidential election took place between

Two young women take a selfie after casting their votes in Texas.

December 15, 1788, and January 7, 1789. It was much different from today's elections. No political parties existed. No one campaigned. George Washington was the choice for president. No one ran against him.

Direct Democracy

This first American presidential election was an important step. It was the first time in history that citizens had voted to elect their nation's leader.

Democracy was not a new idea. In 507 BCE, a man named Cleisthenes created the world's first democracy. It was in Athens, Greece. Male citizens age 18 and older could participate. Women, slaves, and foreigners were excluded. The men met approximately once a week at an assembly called the Ecclesia.

At the Ecclesia, the men voted on each issue and law themselves. This is called direct democracy. Direct democracy works best with small groups. Today, people use it in events such as town meetings. Town meetings are common in only a few states. There,

A modern bust of Cleisthenes, on display at the Ohio Statehouse in Columbus, Ohio

citizens vote directly on items such as budgets, taxes, or town planning.

Indirect Democracy

Direct democracy is not practical for a whole nation. It would take too long for all citizens to vote on every law. Instead, most nations are indirect democracies. Citizens vote for representatives. The representatives then vote on behalf of the people. The United States uses indirect democracy. So does Canada and most of Latin America and Europe.

Throughout the world, citizens use different types of indirect democracy. In the United States, citizens vote for lawmakers and

Young Voters

Twelve thousand American citizens turn 18 every day. This is the age when Americans can vote. For years, fewer younger people have voted than older ones. In 1990, a group called Rock the Vote sought to change that. Rock the Vote uses pop culture to encourage voting. It also uses social media. It has registered more than 6 million new voters.

Donald Pullen, also known as Rockie Fresh, performs during a 2012 tour for Rock the Vote, an organization created to get out the youth vote.

the president. In the United Kingdom and Germany, people elect the lawmakers. Then the lawmakers choose a president or prime minister.

Democracy gives people a say in their government. In 1806, President Thomas Jefferson expressed his confidence in the American people to pick leaders. He said, "Should things go wrong at any time, the people will set them to rights by the peaceable exercise of their elective rights."

Franklin D. Roosevelt served four terms as president. He served longer than any other president in history. In 1938 he spoke about democracy to people in Marietta, Ohio. He said:

Let us not be afraid to help each other—let us never forget that government is ourselves and not an alien power over us. The ultimate rulers of our democracy are not a President and Senators and Congressmen and Government officials but the voters of this country.

Source: Franklin D. Roosevelt. "Address at Marietta, Ohio." The American Presidency Project. *Gerhard Peters and John T. Woolley, n.d. Web. Accessed February 1, 2016.*

What's the Big Idea?

Roosevelt reminds people to help each other. What kind of help is he referring to? How do citizens factor into that help? Are these ideas still relevant today?

CHAPTER TWO

CANDIDATES AND CAMPAIGNS

A person who runs for office is called a candidate. Each candidate has his or her own reasons for running. Some feel a sense of duty. They want to serve their city, state, or nation. Others are unhappy with the way the government is working. They want to change it.

Progressive Party candidate Theodore Roosevelt speaks to New Jersey voters in 1912 during his campaign for president.

Requirements for Office

Candidates for office must meet specific requirements. The US Constitution sets guidelines for the president. The president must be a natural-born citizen. He or she must have lived in the United States for at least 14 years. The president must also be at least 35 years old.

The Constitution also has requirements for members of Congress. Both senators and representative must live in the state they represent. Senators must be at least 30 years old. They must have been US citizens for nine years. Representatives must be at least 25 years old. They must have been US citizens for seven years. State offices have requirements too. They vary from state to state.

Political Parties

Most candidates belong to either the Republican Party or Democratic Party. Each party has different ideas about how to govern. Republicans generally believe in limited government. They are called

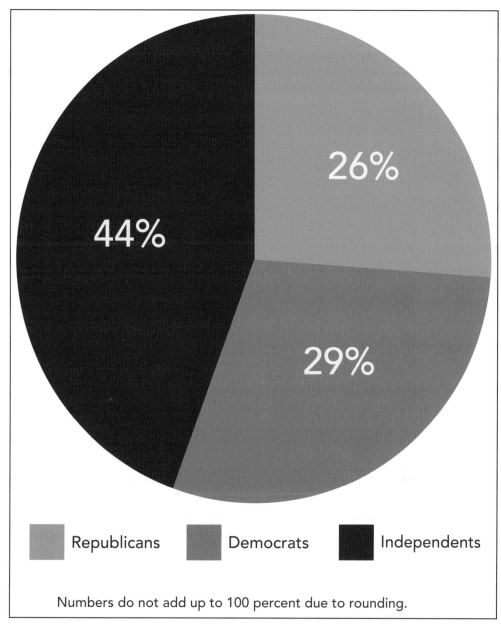

26%

44%

29%

■ Republicans ■ Democrats ■ Independents

Numbers do not add up to 100 percent due to rounding.

Political Party Affiliations of Americans

This pie chart shows the political party affiliations of Americans based on a survey by the Gallup research company in early January 2016. Does the information in the chart add to your understanding of the text in this chapter?

Special Elections

Not all elections are about choosing leaders. Sometimes a referendum appears on the ballot. It allows voters to decide a specific issue. A school district may request a tax increase to fund new computers. Voters can approve or deny the request.

Voters may also take part in recall elections. These are legal in approximately one-third of US states and 60 percent of US cities. A recall happens when citizens want an official to be removed from office. Voters decide if the person should be removed. If the recall is successful, voters select a replacement.

conservatives. Democrats generally believe in a more powerful government. They are called liberals.

Before an election, a candidate joins the party that is closest to his or her beliefs. Several people from one party often want to run for the same office. To choose a candidate, party members meet in each state. They pick a candidate in a primary election or caucus. The winner then runs in a general election.

The process to elect the president is different.

Illinois US Senate candidate Barack Obama speaks in Chicago, Illinois, in 2004.

Each party holds a national convention. It is a four-day meeting where the party officially nominates a candidate. The nominee accepts with a speech. Then the campaign for the general election begins.

Campaigns

A campaign is an effort to win over voters. Candidates travel in the area they represent. Presidential candidates travel throughout the country. Other candidates travel in their home cities and states.

While campaigning, candidates explain what they would do if elected. A candidate might share a plan for creating new jobs. Voters may want a new city park. So a candidate might explain how he or she would raise the money for it.

Candidates often appear on television and radio programs. They may use newspaper ads to share their ideas. Candidates also use websites, Facebook pages, and Twitter accounts.

CHAPTER THREE

ELECTION DAY

The US Constitution allows each state to run its own elections. Some states require photo identification to vote. Others do not. People must register to vote before the election in some states. In other states, people may register on Election Day.

A man holds an "I voted" sticker after casting his ballot in San Francisco, California, in 2012.

Choosing a Date

The general election takes place on the first Tuesday after the first Monday in November. Congress chose this day. Back in the 1800s, many Americans were farmers. Officials did not want the election to interfere with their harvest or travel time. Weather was another concern. Most Americans lived far from their polling places. Many had to travel at least two days to get there and back. The first Tuesday in November gave farmers all day Monday to travel. They could then vote on Tuesday and return home.

Polling Places

People go to their polling place on Election Day. This is where they vote. People usually go to a specific polling place. It is determined by where they live. A polling place can be any public or private building. It may be a local church, a school, or fire station.

Trained staff work at the polling place. They are known as poll workers. In some places they are also called election judges or election inspectors. They make sure that elections are run fairly and smoothly. They set up voting

A voter casts his ballot at a launderette being used as a polling station in San Francisco.

A ballot is fed into a scanner in Brooklyn, New York.

equipment. They hand out ballots. They also register new voters. Most poll workers are paid for their work.

Each political party also has unpaid volunteers at the polling site. They are called poll watchers or monitors. They are there to make sure no one votes who is not supposed to vote. They can make a formal challenge if they suspect fraud.

Ballots

Names of registered voters appear on an official list. Each voter's name is checked off as he or she arrives at the poll. Voters then receive ballots. This is what they will use to vote. Voting is done in secret. The voter enters a booth or other enclosed space. He or she casts a vote in private.

Paper ballots are used in many states. Voters mark their choices with a pen. Different styles of ballots are used. Voters may color in a circle or draw a line. They place the ballots in a scanner. It records the votes.

Digital ballots are also common. Voters use a touch screen, mouse, or keyboard to mark their choices. Votes are recorded directly on the computer in some states. In other states, voters receive a token or receipt. They place it in a ballot box to be counted.

Absentee ballots are another way to vote. Generally, Americans living abroad and elderly citizens vote this way. College students and soldiers can also cast absentee ballots. They must request a ballot from their home state. They mark their choices on the ballot. Then they mail it back to the state.

The Results

Election workers review the ballots. They make sure everything is counted correctly. Then the results are given to the state's secretary of state. He or she collects the results from the entire state. The secretary of state officially announces which candidates won.

EXPLORE ONLINE

Rock the Vote is an organization that encourages young citizens to vote. Go to the website listed below, and click on your state. Find out where your polling place is located. Look at your state's voting requirements. Do you need to show identification to vote? Can you register on Election Day?

Find Your Polling Place

mycorelibrary.com/voting-and-elections

CHAPTER FOUR

THE ELECTORAL COLLEGE

Early American leaders had to decide how the president would be elected. Some wanted the US Congress to elect the president. Others wanted state lawmakers to choose. Another group wanted citizens to elect the president directly.

The framers settled on a compromise. It is a system called the Electoral College. It is an indirect method of electing the president and vice president.

Senate pages arrive in the House chamber carrying sealed certificates to be announced by the Electoral College on January 4, 2013.

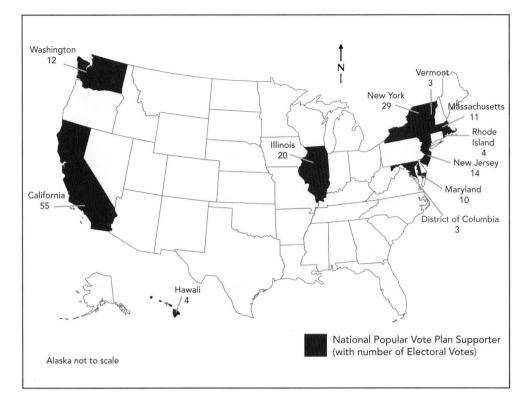

Washington
12

Vermont
3

New York
29

Massachusetts
11

Rhode
Island
4

Illinois
20

New Jersey
14

California
55

Maryland
10

District of Columbia
3

Hawaii
4

National Popular Vote Plan Supporter
(with number of Electoral Votes)

Alaska not to scale

The End of the Electoral College?

This map shows the 11 supporters of the National Popular Vote plan. This plan would guarantee the presidency to the candidate who receives the most popular votes in all 50 states and Washington, DC. How does this graphic help you better understand the information in the text?

The Founding Fathers outlined how it works in the US Constitution.

Each state and the District of Columbia get electors. They get one elector for every representative and senator they send to the US Congress. The total number of electors is 538. For a candidate to win, he or she must have more than one-half of these electors' votes. This means a candidate needs at least 270 electoral votes to win.

Electors

Each state can select its electors however it likes. They are usually chosen at conventions held by political parties in each state. Electors pledge to vote for a specific candidate. An elector chosen at a Republican convention would pledge to vote for the Republican candidate.

When citizens go to the polls on Election Day,

PERSPECTIVES
The National Popular Vote

In 2006, a campaign to change the way the president is elected began. It is called the National Popular Vote plan. Under the plan, states would promise their electoral votes to the candidate who wins the national popular vote. This system would guarantee that the candidate who wins the popular vote would also win the presidency. The plan needs 270 electoral votes to succeed. So far 10 states and the District of Columbia have agreed to the plan. Together, the 11 have 165 electoral votes.

they are actually voting for electors. The names of the electors appear on the ballot by the name of the candidate in some states. In other states, only the candidate's name appears on the ballot. In both cases, the voter is choosing the elector who is pledged to the candidate.

Popular Vote vs. Electoral Vote

Four times in US history, a candidate has won the popular vote but lost the electoral vote. The most recent time was in 2000. George W. Bush and Al Gore ran against each other. Gore won the popular vote. Bush won the electoral vote. He became president. The other three times this happened were in 1824, 1876, and 1888.

Making It Official

When the election is over, the results are announced. These results are called the popular vote. It reflects whom citizens chose for president. Winning the popular vote does not make a candidate the winner of the election. He or she must have at least 270 votes in the Electoral College.

Electors in each state meet on the first Monday after the second Wednesday in December. The electors meet in their home states. It is then that the electors vote. A candidate who wins the popular vote in a state also wins all the state's electoral votes. The only exception to this is in Maine and Nebraska. In those states, electors vote based on the share of popular votes the candidates get.

After the electors vote, the results are recorded. Each state sends its results to the US Congress. On January 6, Congress meets to tally the votes. The vice president announces the results.

On January 20, the new president is inaugurated. Lawmakers, justices, and other leaders gather at the US Capitol in Washington, DC. The chief justice of the Supreme Court delivers the Oath of Office to the newly elected president. Once the president takes the oath, he or she is the nation's new leader.

CHAPTER FIVE

THE RIGHT TO VOTE

Today, most US citizens who are at least 18 can vote in federal, state, and local elections. This was not always the case. When the nation was new, only white men age 21 and older who owned property could vote. As a result, only 6 percent of Americans could vote in the first US presidential election in 1789.

Despite being too young to vote themselves, two Colorado teens help get out the vote in 2008.

The right to vote slowly expanded. Former slaves, Native Americans, immigrants, and women received the right to vote. To guarantee voting rights, Congress and the states amended the Constitution. Today, more than one-third of the Constitution's amendments focus on voting rights.

African-American Voters

The US Congress ratified the Fifteenth Amendment in 1870. It protected the voting rights of former slaves. They could not

36

An 1870 print celebrating the passage of the Fifteenth Amendment to the US Constitution

be denied the right to vote because of their race or because they had been slaves.

Despite this, former slaves faced problems at the polls. Many faced violence if they tried to vote. Some states charged a poll tax. It required voters to pay before they could vote. Sometimes voters had to pass a reading test. Many former slaves were poor and could not read. The violence, taxes, and tests made voting nearly impossible for them.

These practices continued until 1964. That year, the states ratified the Twenty-Fourth Amendment. It outlaws poll taxes. Then, in 1965, Congress passed the Voting Rights Act. It prevents states from discriminating at the polls. After the act passed, more than 250,000 African Americans registered to vote for the first time.

Citizenship

Many other minority groups also had to fight for the right to vote. The challenge they faced was becoming citizens. Laws from the 1800s and early 1900s prevented some immigrants and Native Americans from becoming citizens. This stopped them from voting.

Native Americans were not citizens for much of the nation's history. In 1924 Congress passed the Indian Citizenship Act. It made all Native Americans US citizens. This opened up the right to vote.

For many years, Asian immigrants were not allowed to become citizens. In 1952 Congress passed the Immigration and Nationality Act. It allowed Asian immigrants to become citizens. With it, a whole new community of voters grew.

Women

Women also had to fight for their right to vote. In 1848 approximately 100 Americans met in Seneca Falls, New York, to talk about women's rights. They wanted better rights for women, including their right to vote.

Changing the laws came slowly. By the early 1900s, women began using new methods to attract attention to their cause. They picketed and held rallies.

When the United States entered World

Elizabeth Cady Stanton

Elizabeth Cady Stanton was an early leader of the women's rights movement. In 1848 she helped organize the nation's first convention on women's rights in Seneca Falls, New York. She also gave speeches and wrote articles. Stanton died in 1902. Her leadership inspired women to stand up for the cause. Women finally won the right to vote in 1919.

US citizens voting for their future leaders

War I (1914–1918), women used it to their advantage. They believed that the best way to make the world safe was to ensure democracy for all citizens at home. Lawmakers agreed. The US Congress approved the Nineteenth Amendment in 1919. The states ratified it in 1920. It gives women the right to vote.

Voting Matters

Voting is one of the most important responsibilities of American citizenship. It allows citizens to choose their leaders and make their voices heard. In the United States, every citizen's vote matters.

On May 17, 1957, civil rights leader Martin Luther King Jr. spoke to a group in Washington, DC, about voting rights:

> *Give us the ballot, and we will no longer have to worry the federal government about our basic rights.*
>
> *Give us the ballot, and we will no longer plead to the federal government for passage of an anti-lynching law . . .*
>
> *Give us the ballot, and we will transform the salient misdeeds of bloodthirsty mobs into the calculated good deeds of orderly citizens.*
>
> *Give us the ballot, and we will fill our legislative halls with men of goodwill . . .*
>
> *Give us the ballot, and we will place judges on the benches of the South who will do justly and love mercy . . .*

Source: Martin Luther King, Jr. "Give Us the Ballot." King Encyclopedia. The Martin Luther King Jr. Research and Education Institute, Stanford University, n.d. Web. Accessed January 29, 2016.

Changing Minds

How does King's speech persuade others to support laws guaranteeing civil liberties, such as voting? What makes King's speech persuasive?

- The United States is an indirect democracy. Its citizens elect leaders to represent them on the local, state, and federal levels of government.
- Candidates who want to run for president, vice president, senator, and representative must meet the requirements listed in the US Constitution.
- The United States has two main political parties, the Democrats and the Republicans. Each party nominates candidates for office.
- Americans elect a president and vice president every four years. The election is held on the first Tuesday after the first Monday in November.
- Each state can run elections in its own way. Voting requirements can vary from state to state, as long as they do not violate the US Constitution.
- When citizens vote for president, the results are called the popular vote. A candidate can win the popular vote but lose the election if he or she does not have enough electoral votes.

- On Election Day, citizens are actually voting for electors in the Electoral College. The electors are the ones who elect the president and vice president.
- For many years, voting rights only extended to male citizens older than the age of 21. African Americans, Native Americans, women, and some immigrants were not allowed to vote.
- The US Congress and states have ratified seven amendments to extend voting rights to more groups.

Tell the Tale

Chapter Five discusses the many groups that were unable to vote when the country was formed. Imagine you are a member of one of those groups—a woman, an enslaved person, a Native American, or an immigrant—and write a letter to a friend explaining your situation. Include some reasons why you would like to vote.

Surprise Me

Chapter Four explains how the Electoral College works. What did you find most surprising about it? Write down three facts about the Electoral College that you didn't know before. Why were these facts surprising?

Dig Deeper

After reading this book, what questions do you still have about voting and elections? Ask a librarian to show you additional resources about the topic. Make a list of three new things you learned after your research.

Say What?

Much of the language in the US Constitution is formal and was common at the time of the nation's founding. Pick an article or amendment from the Constitution that has to do with voting rights and rewrite it in today's language. Use a dictionary to look up any words that are unfamiliar.

GLOSSARY

affiliation
a close connection with a group or member

amend
to change or improve something, such as a document

caucus
a closed meeting of members of a political party, usually to select candidates

compromise
the settling of a disagreement by each side giving something up

conservative
a person or idea that generally supports limited government

draft
to select people for mandatory military service

inaugurate
to welcome a person into a high office with a special ceremony

liberal
a person or idea that generally supports a large central government

nominate
to suggest a person for an office or position

primary election
an election to select candidates to run for public office

LEARN MORE

Books

Freedman, Russell. *Because They Marched.* New York: Holiday House, 2014.

Furi-Perry, Ursula. *Constitutional Law for Kids.* Chicago, IL: American Bar Association, 2013.

Jackson, Carolyn. *The Election Book.* New York: Scholastic, 2012.

Websites

To learn more about American Citizenship, visit **booklinks.abdopublishing.com**. These links are routinely monitored and updated to provide the most current information available.

Visit **mycorelibrary.com** for free additional tools for teachers and students.

INDEX

ABOUT THE AUTHOR

Kate Conley is the author of more than 20 nonfiction books for young readers. She lives in Minnesota with her husband and two children.